Animal Crossing: New Horizons - Happy Home Paradise Complete Guide

HELMER LUD

ISBN: 979-8-7603-4645-2

CONTENTS

Happy Home Paradise is the first and potentially only purchasable DLC for Animal Crossing: New Horizons. With it comes a slew of new home design features, items, special currency, and actions exclusive to the DLC. Learn all about designing vacations homes, the Paradise Planning Team, and more with this guide.

Animal Crossing: New Horizons - Happy Home Paradise wiki strategy guide includes everything you need to know about crafting, gaining Nook Miles, and earning money (bells) so you can expand your house, unlock everything, upgrade facilities / shops, and get more resident (villagers) to join your island.

Our Animal Crossing: New Horizons - Happy Home Paradise guide will help you get the most out of grinding for resources, filling your critterpedia with all the bugs and fish you can find while designing, customizing, and shopping to make this island everything you want it to be.

Whether you're a beginner - making this your first-ever Animal Crossing game - or you're a veteran who has their island all planned out: we have important info, tips and tricks, and fun cheats and secrets to enhance your island getaway!

Happy Home Paradise gives players the opportunity to design custom vacation homes for all of their favorite Animal Crossing: New Horizons characters, but it goes far beyond that with unique features that create endless possibilities.

In addition to being a DLC for New Horizons, Happy Home Paradise is also something of a spin-off. Animal Crossing: Happy Home Designer is a full game developed and released in 2015 for the Nintendo 3DS featuring the same premise. Happy Home Designer was never a part of the main Animal Crossing series, but it was the first Animal Crossing game compatible with amiibo, and it allowed players to express their creativity in ways mainline Animal Crossing games didn't. Happy Home Paradise expands on that idea and seamlessly integrates it with Animal Crossing: New Horizons.

Happy Home Paradise DLC Features

The premise of Happy Home Paradise is straightforward: players learn of an opportunity to "go to work" as a vacation home designer in an archipelago made up of several different islands. Through a local resort-planning company called Paradise Planning, players can consult with villagers to learn what their dream home looks like.

Following the consultation, players are given full creative license over the villager's vacation home with seemingly endless customization options. Players are responsible for both the interior and exterior of the vacation home, and can even customize the season and weather. Happy Home Paradise comes with a built-in inventory so that players aren't limited by their own resources. Building inventory can take forever in New Horizons, so it's great to know that grinding won't be necessary.

Players can encounter clients organically in the DLC, but it's also compatible with amiibo if there are specific villagers that players want to design for. Completed vacation homes can be showcased through the Happy Home Network app, which can also be used to tour other players designs for inspiration similar to Dream Addresses in New Horizons.

Finally, players can be assured that they aren't working for free. Designing vacation homes can earn players Poki, a special currency that can only be used in the archipelago. With Poki, players can buy exclusive "rare" items and furniture to bring back to their own islands.

Unique Decorating Opportunities in Happy Home Paradise

A lot of new decorating options are being added to Animal Crossing: New Horizons with the 2.0 update also coming on November 5, but there are some options exclusive to Happy Home Paradise. Just like in New Horizons, players will be able to add accent walls and ceiling lights. For villagers wanting to be roommates, players can also decorate with partitions to divide up a room. Rooms can then be customized with mood lighting and soundscapes.

The DLC adds a lot of quality-of-life updates that completely change the pace of home design. Furniture items can be customized in the moment while decorating a room, and the exterior design tools are more efficient than what New Horizons players are used to. Fences, paths, plants, and items can be easily moved with a grid system just like in the home's interior, which will make things easier. The houses themselves can also be moved without having to get a construction permit in advance from Tom Nook. Rooms can also be resized to suit the villager's style.

How Happy Home Paradise Affects New Horizons

One of the best things about Happy Home Paradise is that the entire DLC doesn't exist separate from the player's main island. Most of the time it does, but after spending time designing vacation homes at the archipelago, players can unlock the opportunity to customize villager homes on their own islands. Some villagers have dreadful interior design skills, so Happy Home Paradise lets players fix all of that.

Customizing villager homes allows players to improve upon a villager's style or completely change it. Starter villagers can greatly benefit from this new feature. The villagers that players start the game with will never have their personalized home, so players often kick their starter villagers out in favor of bringing in a new one with a personalized home. With Happy Home Paradise this won't be an issue any longer, and those starter villagers may have a fighting chance. The DLC will also allow players to bring back exclusive items to decorate their islands.

New Happy Home Paradise NPCs

There are three new NPCs that come with Happy Home Paradise. Fans might already be familiar with Lottie, the otter who worked as a receptionist in Happy Home Designer and walked the player through its tutorial process. Lottie is also present in New Leaf and Pocket Camp as an employee of Happy Home Academy, and she'll be helping the player out in Happy Home Paradise.

The other two NPCs are Niko the monkey and Wardell the manatee. Both Niko and Wardell are new to the Animal Crossing series and are exclusive to Happy Home Paradise. The specific responsibilities of Lottie, Niko, and Wardell aren't exactly clear, but each will play a role in supporting the player on their quest to become a vacation home designer.

HOW TO GUIDES

New Design Features

As you become more experienced with designing Vacation Homes, you'll begin to unlock all-new design techniques that are unique to the Happy Home Paradise update. These all-new design features include:

Changing Room Sizes:-

Change the size of the inside as you increment or diminishing the width and length of a room.

Parcel Walls:-

Parcel dividers can be utilized to separate the space in a room.

Counters:-

Counters can be put at two unique statures.

Columns:-

Make rooms somewhat more sensible as you present roof upholds as columns.

Lighting:-

Lighting can likewise be utilized to change the general mind-set of the room. Regardless of whether it be the shading or by and large brilliance, picking the right lighting has never been more basic to a plan's general feel.

Soundscapes:-

Got a specific topic as a top priority - a Construction site, a Park, or even a Stadium? Give your plan a soundscape to establish the general vibe of the form.

Cleaning:-

Make certain to clean your furniture with care to get a remarkable cleaning impact that givesto your inside plan that final detail it might require.

Paradise Planning Special Furniture

At the end of a hard day, return back to the Happy Home Paradise Planning office to receive compensation for the day's work - the Happy Home Paradise Planning Team uses Poki as its official currency.

So how can you spend your hard-earned money? Well, you'll find a shop within the office that sells rare and special furniture that is otherwise hard to find on your island.

All Special and Rare Furniture Available

Below is a complete list of all special and rare furniture that's available to purchase in the Paradise Planning Office store. Our list will include images, item names, and its cost price in Poki.

Note: While it is not currently confirmed, it appears that the Paradise Planning Office store will rotate on a daily basis.

Item Name	Poki Cost
Schefflera 	990 Poki
Mirror 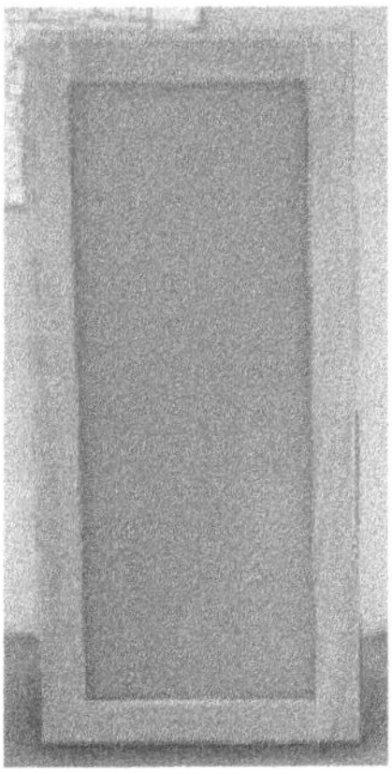	TBA
Sun Chair with Umbrella	TBA

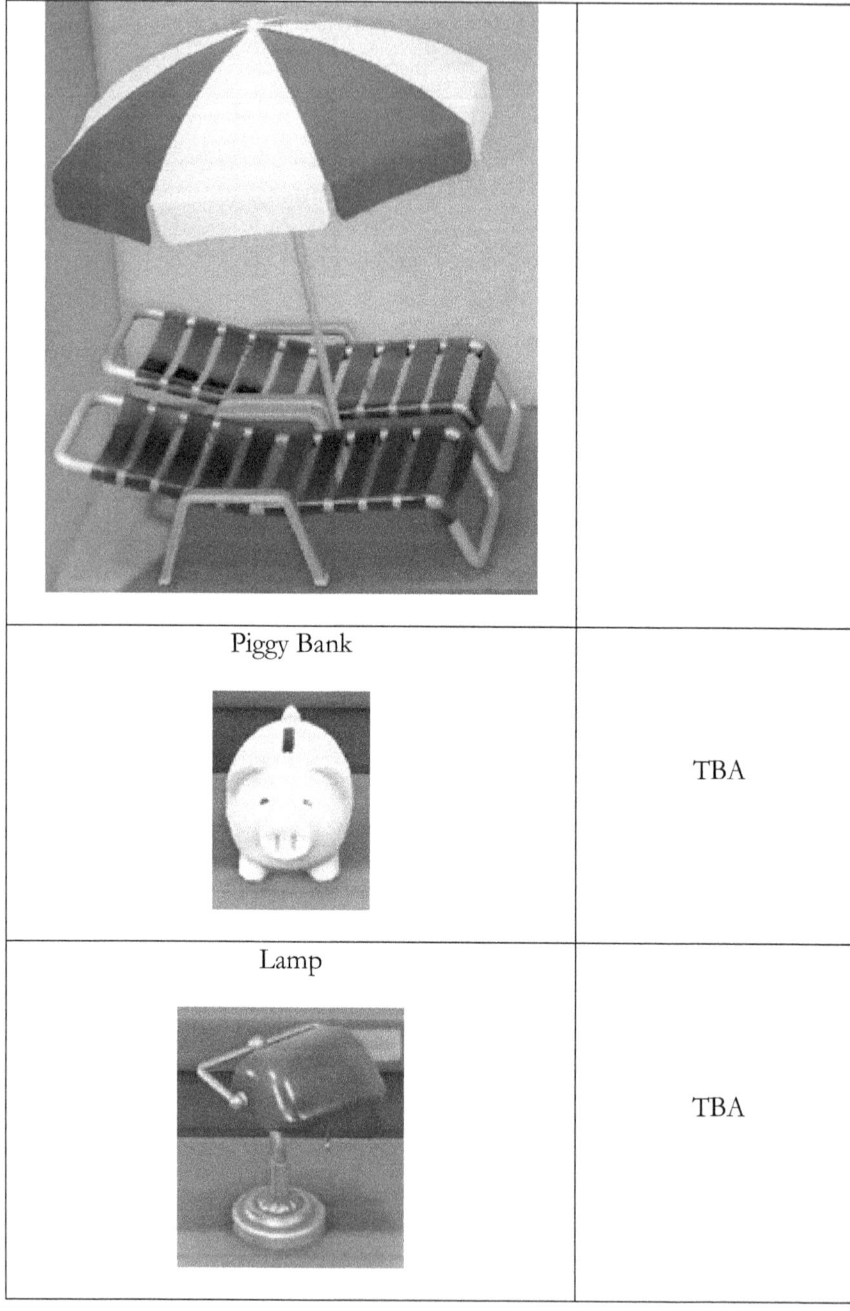	
Piggy Bank	TBA
Lamp	TBA

Roommates

As you progress as a designer, you'll not only unlock new furniture, but you'll also be able to make more suggestions and recommendations to your clients. Among the list of new recommendations, you'll be able to suggest that two clients share a vacation home as roommates.

At this stage, no further details have been revealed about roommates or if they will have any unique features, so be sure to check back on November 5 as we update the page with all the latest details.

Happy Home Network App

Vacation homes that you design can be captured in photos as design samples, which are then recorded in the Paradise Planning portfolio.

To view the portfolio, open the menu on your phone and navigate to the Happy Home Network application in the bottom right corner.

How to Share and View Designs on Happy Home Network App

When using the Happy Home Network application, you can visit previous clients' homes and catch up on how they're doing following your makeover.

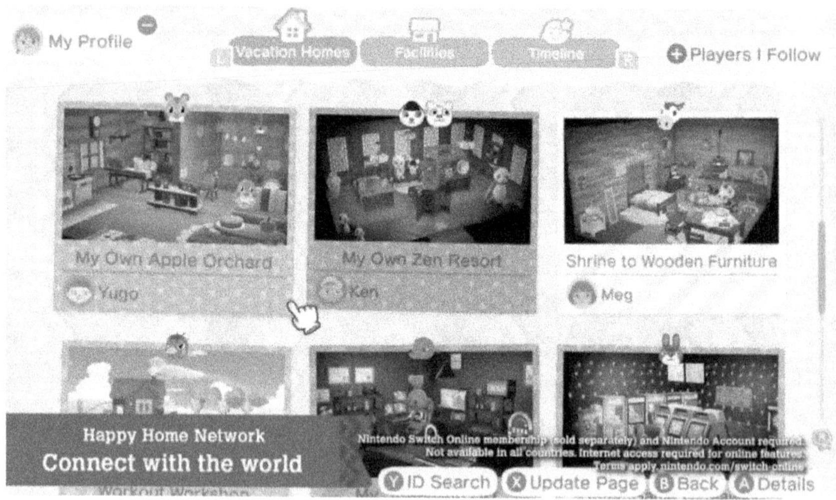

That's not all though, with an active online subscription, you'll have the ability to connect the Happy Home Network online. Here, you can share and view Vacation Home designs and Facility designs from ACNH players all over the world and follow other designers that may inspire you.

Once you have found a design you like, click on it and select Tour, where you'll then have the chance to take an in-person look at their designs and hopefully spark some inspiration of your own.

Soundscapes

What are soundscapes?

Soundscapes are additional background noises players can add while designing vacation homes for NPC villagers in the new, paid DLC update. You'll be able to add sounds like ocean waves, construction noise and more that fit the style and ambience of the home.

You'll also be able to unlock soundscapes to use in your own home on your island, adding soundscapes to your room design any time you like.

Designing Facilities

What facilities can I design in Animal Crossing: New Horizons?

We'll keep this page updated as we learn more about the DLC drop, but we do already know players can design schools, hospitals and restaurants on Lottie's island.

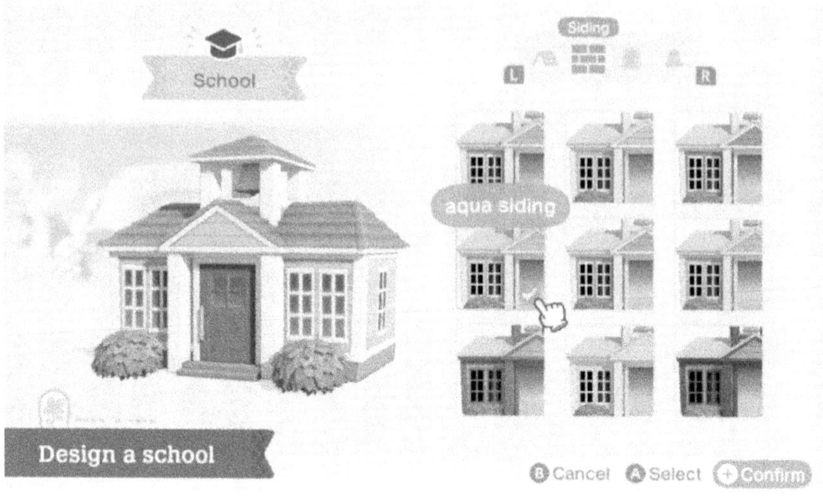

It's unclear if there will be multiple of each facility yet, or if there will only be one of each.

How to design facilities in Animal Crossing

Stay tuned for more information and tips as we learn more about designing facilities!

HOW TO UNLOCK HAPPY HOME PARADISE

After purchasing and downloading the DLC, players will receive a phone call from Tom Nook after starting the game. He will invite you to the airport to meet someone. That someone is Lottie, who previously appeared in Animal Crossing: Happy Home Designer and returns now to help players design facilities and vacation homes for villagers.

After the phone call, you'll automatically be transported to the Dodo Airlines airport, where Lottie will offer you a job designing these buildings on a nearby archipelago (which is a group of small islands).

Accept Lotti's offer and when you're ready, return to the airport and tell Orville, "I want to go to work." Orville will put you on a special flight to Lottie's shop on the archipelago. As you fly over, you'll see photos of the islands you'll soon be exploring and decorating for clients, and they include winter islands, islands with Vines and Glowing Moss, and more.

After you arrive at the archipelago, you'll meet Niko, a small lemur NPC, who will greet you. Follow him to Lottie's office. Once inside Lottie will give you a quick rundown and welcome you to the staff. Congrats, you've unlocked Happy Home Paradise and are about to start designing!

There's a lot to learn and unlock, so you may want to check out the How To Guides hub to learn How to Earn More Poki, for example.

ACNH 2.0 UPDATE

The Animal Crossing: New Horizons 2.0 Update includes a number of locations like The Roost, activities like cooking and stretching with villagers, new island customization through Island Ordinances, and plenty more. Here you'll find everything you need to know about the new features added with the ACNH 2.0 Update.

The 2.0 Update is out. This guide has everything we know about the update so far and will be continuously updated with information Check out the Happy Home Paradise Guide for more information about the upcoming paid DLC launching alongside this massive update.

The Roost and Brewster Return

The 2.0 update will bring back Brewster's Cafe, otherwise called The Roost. Brewster is a non-playable pigeon character previously presented in Animal Crossing: Wild World. In New Horizons you'll have the option to welcome residents and NPCs utilizing the amiibo Call Center, partake in some espresso solo and visit with NPCs and townspeople like Isabelle when they visit the bistro, as well—which will be open all day, every day.

The Roost will be situated in the gallery, and in spite of the fact that gyroids are returning the game, it's not satisfactory if Brewster will store them as he did in past renditions of Animal Crossing.

Brewster's Cafe: The Roost

When is Brewster's Cafe Coming?

Brewster's Cafe, which serves espresso to townspeople and NPCs, is accessible now as a feature of the free 2.0 update. Look at our How to Download the 2.0 Update page for additional subtleties on getting the delivery!

The sign displayed in the video says The Roost will likewise be open all day, every day. Brewster's bistro is situated in the generally existing exhibition hall, so players won't have to reconfigure or change their towns to oblige another structure.

The most effective method to Find Brewster and Get The Roost

In the wake of downloading the free 2.0 update, players should look for Brewster to convey Blather's message about opening up a new bistro. You can find Brewster on the uncommon, new island visits Kap'n is giving occupants.

What would players be able to do in the new Roost Cafe with Brewster?

You'll have the option to visit Brewster at The Roost and partake in some espresso, which will cost 200 Bells as it did in past variants of the game.

You'll likewise have the option to talk with NPC townspeople like Isabelle, who can visit The Roost while you're there, despite the fact that it's not satisfactory in case you'll serve them espresso yourself like players did in Animal Crossing: City Folk.

Players can likewise utilize the amiibo Call Center to welcome characters the bistro, including townspeople and non-residents like the Able Sisters. In the immediate, we learned they might carry organization with them too.

To wrap things up, players will actually want to welcome companions from different islands, and they can come over The Roost and have some espresso together.

Step by step instructions to Use Amiibo at the Roost

Players can utilize the amiibo Call Center inside Brewster's bistro to welcome characters the bistro, including residents and non-townspeople like the Able Sisters. In the immediate, we learned they might carry organization with them too.

How did Brewster and The Roost show up in past Animal Crossing games?

Brewster is a non-playable pigeon character originally presented in Animal Crossing: Wild World, delivered for Nintendo DS in 2005. Players would have to converse with Brewster a few times prior to having the option to buy some espresso for 200 Bells.

Players could likewise arrange espresso drinks for different townspeople, who might stop into the bistro, just as appreciate music by DJ K.K. Since K.K. Slider has a show series in the court in Animal Crossing: New Horizons, it's indistinct whether he will get back to The Roost.

In past titles, Brewster likewise put away the melodic furniture things called gyroids at The Roost. Despite the fact that it's been affirmed that gyroids are returning in New Horizons, it doesn't create the impression that they'll be put away The Roost.

New Villagers

Nine spic and span locals and seven returning residents were uncovered as a component of the Animal Crossing Amiibo Card Series 5 declaration, which occurred during the Animal Crossing Direct on October 15, 2021.

The accompanying new townspeople were flaunted:

Ione (new)

Sasha (new)

Tiansheng (new)

Shino (new)

Marlo (new)

Petri (new)

Cephalobot (new)

Quinn (new)

Chabwick (new)

Zoe (returning)

Expert (returning)

Rio (returning)

Frett (returning)

Azalea (returning)

Roswell (returning)

Confidence (returning)

We didn't recognize some other new locals in the direct, however there's a possibility Nintendo didn't show other new residents coming to ACNH.

Permanent Ladder Set Up Kits

Gone are the times of continually expecting to take out your Ladder to investigate regions that are generally hindered by bluffs! Presented as a feature of the ACNH 2.0 update, players will actually want to get an all-new formula to create Ladder Set-Up Kits, which will go about as a long-lasting stepping stool structure that can be put close by precipices.

To look further into buying the Ladder Set-Up Kit formula and making the various sorts of extremely durable Ladders, make certain to visit our total aide on How to Get a Ladder.

How to Get a Ladder

To get the Ladder, you must progress through Tom Nook's tasks of paying off your tent payment and building your home, building Nook's Cranny, and then a bridge to start work on the three villager homes that need furnishing.

After placing the lots down, Tom Nook will inform you that one recipe will require use of the flowers atop the island's peaks, and will give you the recipe to make a Ladder.

The Ladder is a tool that will allow you to climb or lower yourself to different elevations on the island without having to use a ramp or incline. Thankfully, just like the Vaulting Pole - it won't break!

How to Craft a Ladder

The table below will list everything from sell price, materials needed, durability, and how to unlock a Ladder in Animal Crossing: New Horizons.

Ladder Type	Sell Price	Materials Needed	How To Unlock	Durability
Ladder	1,440 Bells	• 4 Wood • 4 Hardwood • 4 Softwood	Speak to Tom Nook after completing a series of tasks.	Unlimited Uses. Item will not break.

How to Get a Ladder Set Up Kit Recipe

Much like the standard Ladder, you'll need to have progressed through Tom Nook's tasks and have successfully built Nook's Cranny to gain the ability to unlock the recipe.

Having purchased your Ladder Set Up Kit, you may be wondering just how you can use it. Firstly, you'll want to head to your desired location and stand by a cliff. Then, open your inventory, click on the ladder kit, and select the option 'Set Next to Cliff' to place it down.

Performing no additional abilities to the standard Ladder tool, the Ladder Set Up Kit simply adds functionality to place ladders down as permanent structures around your island.

How to Craft All Set Up Ladder Set Up Kits

The table below will list everything from sell price, materials needed durability, and how to unlock all Ladder Set Up Kits in Animal Crossing New Horizons.

Ladder Set Up Kit Type	Sell Price	Materials Needed	How To Unlock	Durability
Ladder Set Up Kit Recipe	NBA	NBA	Purchase the recipe from Nook's Cranny for 2,000 Bells	Unlimited Uses. Item will not break

New Island Customization Options

The 2.0 update will incorporate numerous new island customization choices, including island mandates. In past games, island mandates implied locals would get up prior, head to sleep later, and a couple of other explicit activities relying upon which law you chose.

Look at the pages beneath for extra data about new island highlights:

Island Ordinances

Island Ordinances originally showed up in Animal Crossing: New Leaf. As Mayor, players could pick statutes that changed residents' practices or made your town more delightful. In New Horizons, the arrival of mandates is comparable and permits you to tweak your play style.

Instructions to Enact Ordinances

At the point when you're prepared to sanction an Island Ordinance, visit Isabelle in Resident Services. On the off chance that you don't have the structure adaptation of Resident Services yet make certain to visit our aide on How to Upgrade Resident Services prior to proceeding. You should likewise have Animal Crossing refreshed to basically Ver. 2.0.0.

Plunk down to talk with Isabelle. Then, at that point, select the accompanying:

Survey island highlights.

Talk about statutes.

Now, Isabelle will advise you regarding any as of now dynamic statutes. Establishing a mandate costs 20,000 Bells, so be ready for this weighty cooperation and recording charge!

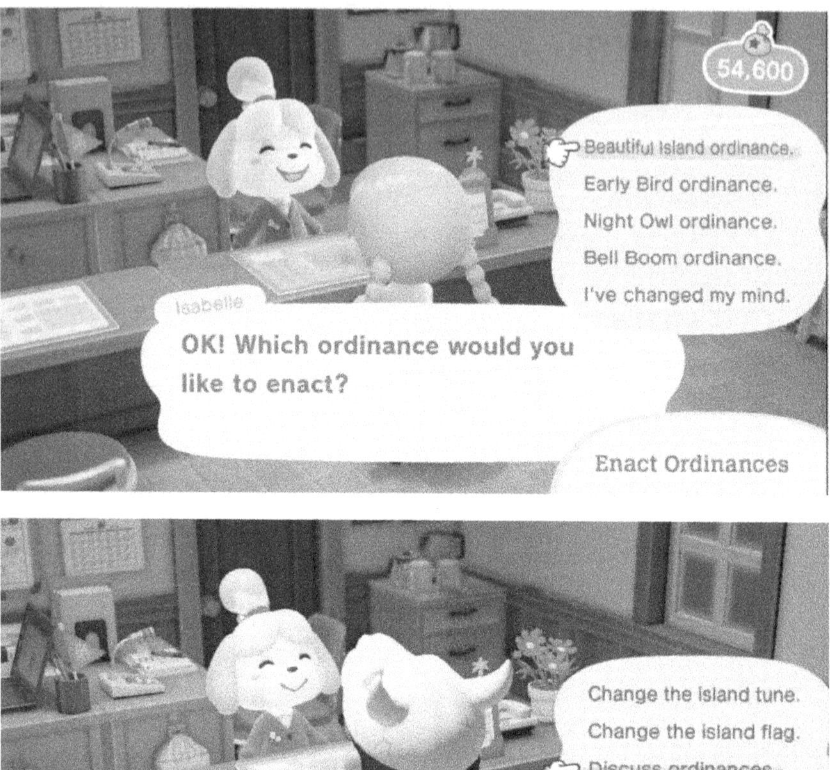

What Island Ordinances Mean for Your Island

You can perceive what every one of the laws means for your island in the graph underneath. For reference, Nook's Cranny is normally open from 8 AM - 10 PM and Able Sisters is open from 9 AM to 9 PM.

ORDINANCE NAME	ORDINANCE EFFECT
Beautiful Island Ordinance	Villagers will assist in clearing weeds, watering flowers, and clearing trash from the water. The Beautiful Island Ordinance could be especially helpful if you plan to do a

	lot of fishing and don't want to deal with tossing trash.
Early Bird Ordinance	Villagers wake up earlier. With the Early Bird Ordinance Nook's Cranny is open from 7 AM - 10 PM and Able Sisters is open from 8 AM - 9 PM.
Night Owl Ordinance	Villagers stay up later. With the Night Owl Ordinance Nook's Cranny is open from 8 AM - 11 PM and Able Sisters is open from 9 AM - 10 PM.
Bell Boom Ordinance	Items cost more but sell for more at shops. To get down to the math, you'll earn an extra 20% for all items you sell. Items at Nook's Cranny and Able Sisters will cost an extra 20%. Strategically, you should only enact the Bell Boom Ordinance if you're planning on selling enough to make back more than you paid for the ordinance and don't plan on buying much. Note that coffee from The Roost and items from Visitors do not increase in price.

After you've picked a law it'll become real the next day.

You can check which law you have dynamic by sitting down with Isabelle at Resident Services and picking the Discuss Ordinance choice once more. She will not charge you assuming all you need to do is see which is dynamic. Assuming you need to drop a law, in any case, that is an alternate story.

Instructions to Remove an Ordinance

If you don't care for your law or need to eliminate it for another explanation, you can change or eliminate a statute by addressing Isabelle in Resident Services. You'll have to have something like 20,000 Bells in your pocket to arrive at the choice.

Once in the menu, you'll see a fourth choice for "Drop our statute." Choosing this will charge you 20,000 Bells. Be certain you truly don't need the statute or would rather really like to have an alternate mandate basically!

Hav's Island Shopping Plaza

Harv's Island is getting a considerable redesign with the Animal Crossing: New Horizons 2.0 Update. A few shopping spots are joining Harv's photograph studio on the distant island and will offer an assortment of administrations alongside another home for some, meeting characters. You'll need to assist with making the shopping region a reality by contributing Bells for each shop.

Make certain to visit the Harv's Island Shopping Plaza page for more data on each shop after the update.

Cooking and New Crops

Cooking is coming to Animal Crossing New Horizons! The 2.0 update will permit players to develop new yields and collect them to cook new plans utilizing kitchenware furniture in your home.

Similar as the game recently presented pumpkins that players could develop, collect and sell, this update will incorporate many new harvests players can use to make the approaching plans. Investigate the Fruits, Vegetables, and Cooking Ingredients page to perceive what we know about new things you can find and develop for cooking plans.

Inquisitive what you'll have the option to cook and what fixings or instruments you really want? Look at the Cooking Guide and Recipes page to perceive what we know about cooking up until now.

Gyroids

Gyroids, the strange minimal melodic furniture animals, are getting back to Animal Crossing: New Horizons! In contrast to past games, it's insufficient to just uncover them. They need to develop for the time being to be reaped. This time around, they'll be adaptable too.

As in past games, gyroids will be more normal after a downpour. To find out additional, check our Gyroid List and Guide page, which will be refreshed with additional data after the new update discharges!

New Furniture and Home Customization

The 2.0 update for New Horizons will incorporate new furnishings and new choices for home customization, including roof stylistic layout and highlight dividers! It's not satisfactory yet how players will open the Pro Decorating License, however that permit is the means by which you'll have the option to add light installations, racking and more to the roofs in your home.

Ceiling Decor

What will roof stylistic theme resemble?

Creature Crossing: New Horizons is getting roof stylistic theme! Players will actually want to hang lights, racks, and different things from their roof with the Pro Decorating License.

This will truly grow the plan capacities inside your home!

When is roof stylistic layout coming to Animal Crossing: New Horizons?

In the October 15, 2021 uncommon Animal Crossing direct, Nintendo reported that the 2.0 update will deliver November 5, 2021. Roof stylistic theme, highlight dividers and the Pro Decorating License will accompany the free update.

What is a Pro Decorating License?

The update hasn't dropped at this point, so it's muddled precisely how players will get the Pro Decorating License. We'll refresh this page as we find out additional! Notwithstanding, already in the game, players needed to finish "Undertaking K" to open terraforming on the island, so it's conceivable the Pro Decorating License will accompany an expense to open it.

Froggy Chair

What is Froggy Chair in Animal Crossing?

In case you're on this page it's impossible you don't definitely know about the image ified, much-cherished Froggy Chair. Also, we can't lie, Froggy Chair fundamentally took the Animal Crossing Direct show.

All things considered, in the event that you haven't heard, Froggy Chair is a charming household item in the Animal Crossing game series. It's a green plastic seat that, all things considered, it resembles a frog. It had been a piece of each game until New Horizons, showing up on GameCube, DS, Wii, and 3DS.

When is Froggy Chair Coming back to Animal Crossing: New Horizons?

In the October 15, 2021 Animal Crossing direct, Nintendo declared the new 2.0 update, which incorporates Froggy Chair. That update drops November fifth, 2021. It shows up behind the scenes during a scene flaunting the new restricted space route in homes.

Froggy Chair recently cost 1,400 Bells, yet it's not satisfactory the amount it will cost in the new game. We'll update you as often as possible! Froggy Chair will likewise be adaptable again this time around, and players can change the shading to yellow, and different shades!

Pause, for what reason is Froggy Chair no joking matter once more?

So back in late 2019, Froggy Chair turned into a Tumblr image and spread all over the web in a lot of healthy and frequently charming jokes. It was one of the additional inspiring images, in case we're being straightforward.

At any rate, fans were quite mooched out when Froggy Chair didn't return in Animal Crossing: New Horizons, and were clamoring to have the furniture thing added back. At long last, it appears Nintendo chose to give Froggy Chair fans what they were absent.

Increased Storage and Improved Movement

Players will actually want to store more things in their homes stockpiling and move all the more effectively around restricted spaces in houses with the new update! There are three new moves up to home stockpiling and the capacity to explore sharp corners with close furniture in your home.

Actually take a look at the pages beneath for more data about New Horizons stockpiling and development refreshes!

Home Storage

How huge is home stockpiling in New Horizons?

Already in New Horizons, home stockpiling was covered at 2,400 things. As per the unique Animal Crossing direct on October 15, 2021, capacity will be redesigned multiple times, to hold upwards of 5,000 things. This will be important for the free, 2.0 update dropping November 5, 2021.

It's not satisfactory yet how much every capacity overhaul will cost, however we'll update you as often as possible as we find out additional!

New Villager Interactions and Player Reactions

The new update will include 11 new reactions like stretch, listening ears, jammin' and more! These will allow players to communicate more in-game and interact in new ways with NPCs and villagers, who will sometimes copy your reaction or react to it.

Check out the Reactions page for more details on these new features!

CHEATS AND SECRETS

Animal Crossing: New Horizons may be a relaxing game about building your island community from the ground up, but that doesn't mean there aren't a wealth of secrets, unlockables, and even a few tricks and cheats to get things done all the better.

Art Museum Time Travel Cheat

Completing the Art Wing of the Museum can be a trying task but if you're tired of wondering when Redd appears and are looking to pick from fake vs. real art fast, you can use this Time Travel Cheat to speed things up. Here's how to do it. Cheat credit to Doug Chin for contacting us about this exploit.

To start with, you'll need Redd on your island. In case Redd is mysteriously absent, Time Travel (change your framework clock) each day in turn until you see him.

Shop at Redd's once he shows up. Utilize our Art Guide to pick the genuine workmanship, rather than the fakes (and monitor them with our intuitive agenda). Relax in case Redd is selling only fakes; you don't have to purchase anything for this cheat to work. Save, leave your game, then, at that point, close the product totally.

Head to System settings on your Switch. Select framework, then, at that point, select Date and Time. Ensure Synchronize Clock through Internet is wound down. Change the Date and Time to go on.

Fire up Animal Crossing. It's another day and Redd is gone. Go ahead and utilize this opportunity to get your craft from the mail and even give it to the gallery in the event that you'd like.

At the point when you're prepared, save, exit, and close the product. Get back to the framework settings and change your clock back to the earlier day to resummon Redd. He'll have new stock in his shop!

Do this process again until your historical center gathering is finished.

Caution: Don't Time Travel Too Far

Remember that on the off chance that you go ahead or back over one day Redd will at this point don't show up. If you see Redd on May thirteenth you can't simply reliably get back to May thirteenth weeks after the fact. We've found it can require as long as about fourteen days for him to show up again so be cautious when utilizing this cheat or you'll have a great deal of time travel work in front of you.

Unbreakable Tools Exploit

Indeed, even ACNH's Golden Tools aren't strong however you can insight and appreciate tough instruments by utilizing this sofa community exploit. As of Nintendo Switch variant 10.0.0, you can remap the Switch buttons. You can set up custom button planning that permits you to control 2 characters on the double (one on each bliss con).

The "Devotee" player's devices never break (as long and they're not changed to being the Leader).

There are a lot of agonies and limits to utilizing this endeavor. For example, Only the pioneer has full admittance to their pockets, can enter structures, shop, and just the pioneer can get products of the soil. Supporters can get fish and bugs yet those will naturally be put away in the reuse receptacle in Resident Services - to be recovered later.

Notwithstanding, it can in any case be a decent way of achieving some every day assignments without stressing over apparatuses blasting immediately and inexplicably. For how to do lounge chair center and how to eliminate an individual from your island (assuming you at any point choose to leave this adventure) look at our How to Play Multiplayer guide.

Stalk Market - Turnip Selling Cheat

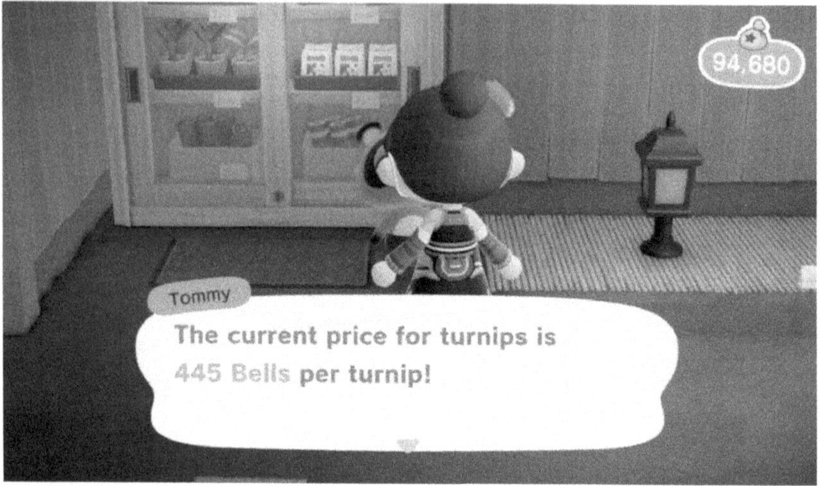

Timmy and Tommy's turnip purchasing costs are randomized each day, and are randomized again on the off chance that you go back in time to purchase more turnips and return - making it difficult to make a person who jumps through time's killing on the tail market. In any event, in your own game.

Here's the manner by which to swindle the tail market and make a huge load of ringers on turnips:

Initial, a companion, or an amicable individual on the web, should screen their turnip costs. At the point when they get an incredible cost, request that they pave the way for you. Perceive How to Play Multiplayer if you really want to figure out how to do this.

Any turnips you as of now have will ruin on the off chance that you turn back the clock, so consider visiting your companion's island and selling them first prior to proceeding with this cheat!

Presently that you're without turnip, change your Nintendo Switch's date and time inside the framework settings. Set it to the past Sunday, any time somewhere in the range of 5am and 12pm.

Buy a huge load of turnips from Daisy Mae, the voyaging hog turnip merchant. Simply fill your pockets with the most that you can.

Go directly to your companion's island with the marvelous turnip purchasing costs. You don't need to change the date on your own Switch!

Sell your turnips. Create significant gain.

You can rehash stages 3 through 5 however many occasions as you need before Nook's Cranny shut in your companion's town (at 10pm)

Remember your companion can't time travel, or, in all likelihood their turnip costs will reset! Leave them a couple of sacks of 99k chimes as much appreciated.

Time Traveling

In what has turned into a staple of taboo Animal Crossing enchantment, New Horizons additionally permits the capacity for players to "time travel". Since the game sudden spikes in demand for the Switch's own inside clock, you can change this check in your control center's settings when not in the game to progress or rewind time to any date you wish.

By time traveling, players can quickly progress by a day to restock their island with new assets, fossils, new things in shops, and quick forward the time taken to develop structures and different elements on the island. Done accurately, a player can accumulate ringers quicker than ordinary or progress their island by getting out ahead a day after most every day errands are finished.

Nonetheless, leaping to far can have unfavorable impacts:

Weeds might become more copious in your nonattendance

Getting out a very long time ahead can trigger player inertia, and cockroaches might show up in your home

Townspeople might feel ignored and leave your island on the off chance that you get out ahead excessively far

Turnips will ruin on the off chance that you leap to another Sunday, or rewind time.

How to Get an In-game ACNH Nintendo Switch

In case you're one of a handful of the players who bought an uncommon Animal Crossing Nintendo Switch, you'll get this message via the post office alongside a present:

" Dear __, Thanks for utilizing the exceptionally hued Joy-Con regulators delivered in relationship with Animal Crossing: New Horizons. To show our appreciation, we're sending you this gift. We trust you appreciate it! - From Nintendo"

The model Animal Crossing: Nintendo Switch can be bought, yet it'll just appear arbitrarily valued at 35,960 ringers.

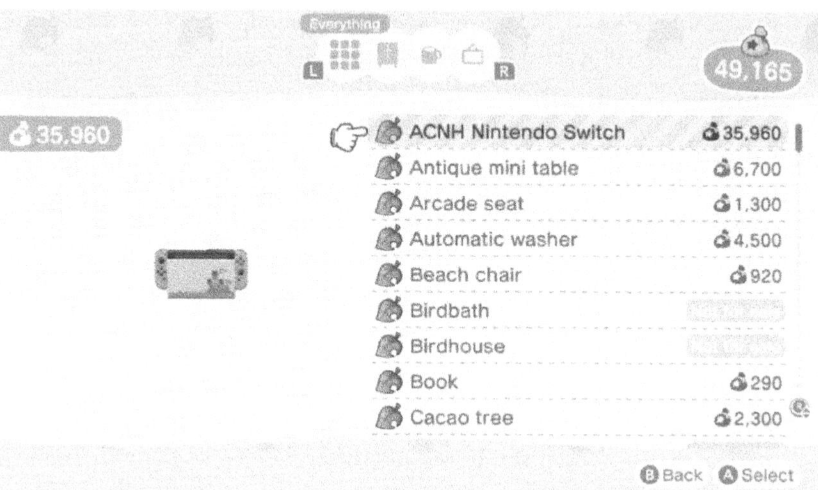

A way of getting around this lofty value is to interface the exceptionally hued Joy-Con to your framework and play ACNH with it. It's not the least demanding workaround, yet on the off chance that you know a companion or relative with a framework, check whether you can acquire them briefly to save 35K Bells.

Get 8 Resources for every Rock

There's a way of ensuring you'll get eight assets for every stone, you simply need to deliberately burrow openings behind you to forestall being thumped back! Position yourself inbetween the stone and the openings, the slam away with your digging tool as quick as possible.

Bell Rocks - How to Score Free Money

Quite a while mystery of the Animal Crossing games, each town is dabbed with rocks in irregular areas, and they can be hit with scoops or even tomahawks to get assets. Nonetheless, every day, one irregular stone will contain ringers rather than minerals, and you can continue to hit it to bring in increasingly more cash. Make certain to prevent yourself from getting thumped back by burrowing openings behind yourself (above/underneath and aside) and strike the stone a limit of multiple times to get up to 16,400 ringers every day!

Glowing Spots - Invest for Bell Trees

Another returning element are strange sparkling spots in the ground that show up in an irregular piece of your island every day. On the off chance that you find this spot, you can uncover it for a free 1,000 chimes. Make certain to gain admittance to a Shovel by giving 5 bugs or fish to Tom Nook and get Blathers to your island.

When you track down a sparkling spot, uncover the ringers - yet realize that on the off chance that you plant the chimes back in the shining opening (and just that gleaming opening), it will grow into a tree that will return 3x the measure of chimes when it's completely developed. You can do this with either 1,000 or 10,000 ringers - which can allow you to make you truckload of cash for your speculation!

See precisely how it's done in the video beneath or on the How to Plant a Money Tree page.

Stopping Wasps in Their Tracks

Nothing is more regrettable than shaking a tree to find a wasp home falling at your feet. You've just got seconds to run into a structure or get your net, however imagine a scenario where you want additional time.

As it would turn out, you can end the Wasp's assault by either opening your stock, or squeezing up on the DPAD for your instrument ring if you've purchased the update from Nook's Shop. With this, you'll have the option to pause for a minute to find and trade to your net - simply be prepared to rapidly turn and swipe to get them before you get stung.

You can likewise keep yourself out of the present circumstance by keeping a net prepared while shaking trees and by just shaking them from the front as displayed in the screen capture beneath. Your person will consequently go to confront the wasps if a home drops, making for a very simple catch!

Borrowing Villager Furniture

Once in a while you might end up far away from your own studio and you're in critical need of another hatchet. Fortunately, numerous Villagers on your island will place DIY Workbenches in their own homes. If one of them is at home, enter, and you'll have the option to utilize it yourself to get what you want!

This additionally works for any mirrors to rapidly change your appearance, as you'll get a greater number of haircuts than what you needed to look over toward the beginning of the game, and you may not find a formula to make your own mirror for some time.

Additionally, if another resident is as of now utilizing their workbench - converse with them and they'll give you the formula for whatever they are chipping away at!

Legendary Rain Fish

Fishing can be all in or all out, in case you're attempting to rake in some serious cash quick. It's difficult to discern whether that huge shadow is a significant fish - or simply a bass, however there are a few different ways to build your opportunities for a fortunate find.

Make certain to consistently fish in the sea when it downpours - as it will offer you a chance at viewing as the absolute most uncommon fish in the game, including the Coelacanth, the ancient fish worth an incredible 15,000 ringers alone!

Terraform Your Own Bridges

When you get far enough into advancing the situation with your island that you open the capacity to terraform and make or eliminate streams, you can utilize this capacity to make modest however compelling extensions.

Ordinarily, you can demand the situation of scaffolds from Tom Nook at Resident Services, yet the costs can get pretty high, and they require a day to construct. Nonetheless, with the Water Tool license you can purchase subsequent to learning the Island Designer App, you can place soil into waterways to make scaffolds of land.

Since your person can bounce over little holes, you can even make little ways to hop across waterways, instead of deterring the stream altogether!

Friends in Other Hemispheres

When beginning the game, you'll be asked which side of the equator you live in - which will direct how the seasons change dependent on where you reside. Walk climate is a lot of a spring climate in the North, while it looks much more like Summer in the South.

This really reaches out to the sorts of bugs and fish you'll find. This implies that while a player in the North will find grouped butterflies in March, a player in the South will find crickets all things being equal. The critterpedia will precisely change the occasions these fauna are found when in that side of the equator - so in the event that you travel to a companion's town in an alternate region of the planet, you can get critters you'd ordinarily need to stand by a lot more months to find in your own town.

It pays to have companions in distant spots!

Secret Crafting Supplies

You'll learn almost immediately that to make a great deal of DIY things, you'll need to gather a ton of branches, wood, stone, iron, and different materials - however a few assets probably won't be simply self-evident.

Contingent upon the plans you uncover, you can likewise find utilizes for arbitrary things like Wasp Nests (to make honeycomb ground surface or medication from), Seashells (to make ocean side covers and shell furniture), and even rubbish fished from the water.

You may likewise find Gold Nuggets that merit a huge load of cash - but on the other hand they're expected to construct some greater DIY Projects, so you may likewise need to cling to a couple. Indeed, even Gulliver's communicator parts that you can uncover to assist him with canning be kept (you beast), as they'll transform into rusted parts the following day and can be utilized to create select ventures you might find.

Villager Be Gone - Getting a Villager to Leave

Everybody has a tale about their ideal town that is attacked by a resident who simply smells. Perhaps you don't care for their character, or their imbecilic expression, or simply disdain Chickens...

Despite your reasons, there is a way of getting Villagers to leave your town, however it takes a touch of devotion, karma, and time.

Try not to be tricked - telling Isabelle you object to a resident won't influence their choice to leave, it is just for resetting their expression and additionally clothing if they have gotten something from another player.

Recollect that most importantly, Villagers need collaborations to feel appreciated, and the less welcome they feel, the almost certain they are to think about leaving. This implies not conversing with them at all whenever the situation allows.

One thing you can do - however it isn't ensured to hurry their takeoff, is either hit them multiple times with a bug getting net, or over and over run into them until they get frantic at you. In the case of nothing else, it's a decent method of communicating your disappointment with them.

The other central concern to know is that townspeople leaving requires some investment. Townspeople will not want to leave an island until there are something like 6 on your island, and it might require a few days for somebody to think about leaving. During this time, make certain to take a gander at your locals - if any of them have an idea bubble over their heads, it implies they are settling on a choice or have an errand. Now and again they'll need something, and some of the time they'll make reference to they might need to leave your town.

If a resident you like has this idea, you can convince them to remain - however assuming its the resident you need out, make certain to empower the choice, and quite soon it will be declared that the resident is getting together to leave.

A left resident will leave behind the part they took over for another person to move in, so make certain to search for somebody to fill the spot before another undesirable resident moves in!

Secret Photo Op Locations

You can utilize photograph mode pretty much anyplace utilizing the Camera application on your in-game NookPhone. Be that as it may, you can get more extensive, more beautiful points by taking photographs in any of the mysterious photograph operation areas. You can perceive you're in one on the grounds that the camera will concentrate in or give a more extensive point.

There are a few in the gallery, including these:

Take a stab at stopping in a couple of spots and see what occurs!

Other Neat Details and Secrets

Some fish show up in various dishes in your home; The seahorse is in a pet tank, while goldfish are in a china bowl.

You can place things in garbage bins.

On the off chance that you put a latrine furniture thing in your home, you can sit on them and receive a little spring up message when you "use" them. This is additionally how you can dispose of organic product you've eaten......

If you leave spoiled turnips on the ground, a path of subterranean insects will show up around them.

Forget about instruments in the open, and Villagers might find and play with them.

In the event that you leave Gulliver's correspondence parts in your pocket, the following day they will end up being an uncommon rusted part making material.

On the off chance that you continue to shake a tree, more branches will drop out.

During the day a little yellow bird can be found on the notice board with another message, while around evening time, an owl roots there.

On the off chance that you show plans for shirts (and even caps) at the Able Sisters, another resident may wear it for some time.

Item Duplication Glitch (Single Switch Co-operation Only)

When playing Animal Crossing with a subsequent player, utilizing the Call Island Resident element, there is right now a way of copying numerous sorts of things, and as soon as possible sell a whole stock of important plunder as quick as you can make more.

Note that this error must be instituted with two players on a solitary Switch console, as on the web or nearby multiplayer doesn't permit visitors to collaborate with put objects, nor can the host get them.

In the first place, bring the subsequent player utilizing Call Resident, and afterward place a high-selling thing on a little table or stool - this can go from little important things to uncommon bugs and fish, or even the Royal Crown sold indiscriminately times from the Able Sisters - which can sell for a gigantic measure of Bells!

When the thing is put on the stool, have the subsequent player (the person who can't get to their stock) hold down A to snatch the table and afterward turn the thing. At the point when this occurs, the principal player should get the thing with Y directly as it turns.

Whenever done effectively, the principal player will take the thing in their stock, while the subsequent player keeps on turning a duplicate of the thing on the table. Whenever adjusted, you can continue to get copies until your stock is full!

TIPS AND TRICKS

Collect DIY Recipes

A significant part of New Horizons is getting together new plans to create out of materials you can gather all around the island. Some you can get from formula books sold by Timmy or the Nook Miles Store, and some are situational - like fishing up junk or conversing with a resident in the wake of getting stung by wasps.

Every day, you'll find no less than one message bottle along the ocean side containing an irregular formula. *You can likewise visit your resident's homes once they move up to houses, and on the off chance that you see them making at their own studio - converse with them and they'll give you the formula for whatever you're chipping away at.

Worn out on taking too long to even consider creating things? Crush the A button to make the cycle speed up!

Continuously make time to kill inflatables with your slingshot (tune in for the blasting breeze), as the presents they hold can contain nearly anything - including more plans!

Plans need a wide range of assets and materials - some of which you may not understand can be utilized, similar to weeds, wasps homes, and shells.

Not everything plans can be modified, but rather once you open the customization studio, you can modify the shade of numerous DIY things, and even add examples to some of them.

Monitor your neighbors whenever they've moved up to houses. They'll at times be chipping away at a formula you don't claim.

When you open the campground, Amiibo guests will demand a thing. They'll give you the DIY formula on the off chance that you don't have it.

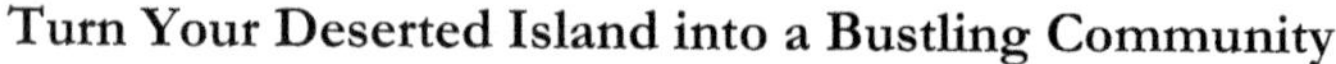

Turn Your Deserted Island into a Bustling Community

You might see your island lacking many provisions during your initial not many days. Things like hourly music, town tunes and town banners will not be accessible until Resident Services can redesign from a tent - so help Tom Nook out with all that you can!

Relax on the off chance that you don't care for where you've put a tent or building - you'll ultimately have the option to move everything aside from Resident Services and the Airport - however be ready to follow through on a cost.

More Villagers will communicate interest in going to your island the better it looks, so begin enlivening your island with open air furniture to develop your rating!

Be ready to spend a ton of Bells assuming you need Timmy and Tommy to redesign their shop - however the compensations of a greater stock and custom instruments are definitely justified. Learn more in the How to Unlock Everything in Animal Crossing: New Horizons guide.

When you're ready to save plots for imminent townspeople - know an irregular resident might guarantee it, regardless of whether you're highly involved with tempting someone else you've to move to your town!

Love Thy Villagers

The more you visit with Villagers, the better companions you'll be - and the more uncertain they'll be to ponder leaving the island.

Assuming you need a particular resident to join your island, search for them on Mystery Islands or at your Campground when you assemble it, and welcome them to remain.

After around 6 days of talking, you'll have the option to give them gifts - and they can give back!

Send Villagers letters or help them with assignments, and they'll remunerate you in kind!

Don't Waste Resources

Your Deserted Island is for all intents and purposes blasting at the creases with trees, shakes, and weeds that can be utilized as making fixings and offered to Timmy and Tommy.

The straightforward demonstration of creating a thing can twofold its worth over the cost of the assets it was produced using

When you help Timmy and Tommy construct Nook's Cranny, they'll proposition to get one "hot thing" each day at twofold its typical worth, which will consistently be an irregular created thing. This implies you can tolerate making four fold the amount of cash than selling weeds or branches for their base worth!

Utilize the Nook Miles Ticket to go to a Mystery Island on the off chance that you wind up running low on provisions, as there will be bounty more trees and shakes to dig for assets.

In case you're coming up short on island assets, consider buying a Nook Miles Ticket to visit a remote location.

At the point when no doubt about it, "A" twice and hold it down to make the creating movement quicker.

Get the Most Out of Rocks

Long-term Animal Crossing fans will thoroughly understand the stones that dab your island. At the point when you prepare a digging tool (or even a hatchet when absolutely necessary), you can strike the stone a few times to gather assets - and an irregular stone every day will drop chimes all things being equal.

The more you strike it rapidly - the more you'll receive in return, and there's a stunt to ensuring you don't get thump supported too far to even consider continueing hitting the stone:

Ensure there's nothing on all sides of the stone you intend to mine. In case weeds are developing, they'll occupy significant room and square the space of the assets you chip away.

Remain at one of the edges of the stone, and burrow two openings on one or the other side of you so they are preventing you from creating some distance from the stone.

In case you are experiencing difficulty calculating your person to strike the stone dead on, you can move into where the openings combine and your person will hop askew over them, and bouncing back will confront you directly at the stone.

Pound the A button to quickly strike the stone up to multiple times. That is extremely sum times you can get assets from a stone each day - which can approach up to 16,400 ringers if you've tracked down the irregular cash rock for the afternoon!

Get Those Miles

When Tom Nook shows you the miracles of Nook Miles, you'll see they can be utilized for everything from taking care of your first advance, to opening more stock space and hairdos, and significantly more.

Make sure to check in at the Resident Services terminal consistently, regardless of whether you just play for a couple of moments. The more days straight you registration, the more miles you'll get - right to 300 miles every day subsequent to checking in for seven days in a row.

Improve Tool Recipes, Tool Ring, and Expanded Inventory when you can by amassing Nook Miles.

Most all Nook Miles Rewards are attached to assignments you'll attempt in any case, so anticipate getting compensated for what you excel at.

Watch out for your Nook Mileage card, as new difficulties will show up as you open more devices and offices, and some of them will not appear until you complete them on mishap - like getting 5 wasps in succession, or losing an inflatable present in the water.

Find and Talk to Visitors

While you'll get a declaration each new day you play - beginning at 5am - one thing they don't educate you concerning are any unique visiting characters on the island that day. Truth be told, you can undoubtedly pass up these characters altogether in case you're not giving your island an exhaustive range, so ensure you search for these vivid characters.

A significant number of them have assignments they need assistance with, or select things to sell, so consistently make certain to check in with them to get important prizes.

The agreeable Ghost Wisp just shows up around evening time, and you'll have to assist get his soul parts with a Net.

Gulliver can appear on an arbitrary piece of your ocean side, and to get him home, you'll need to dive for communicator parts in the sand that are veiled as shellfishes (search for the water letting out).

Mabel just comes to sell her products after you fabricate Nook's Cranny, yet if you spend enough ringers on her apparel, she might request to open up shop for all time!

Prattles' sister Celeste can appear the evening of a meteor shower (pay attention to your residents on the off chance that they notice a starry evening), and she'll tell you the best way to make an enchanted wand from meteorite parts you can wish on when gazing upward into the sky and squeezing An on a falling star. Check out the shore the following day for your prize!

Catch Bugs and Fish

Different Fish and Bugs are found on your island depending on everything from the time of day, the weather, and the month.

Some bugs won't show themselves unless certain conditions are met. Try chopping trees to create stumps, leave out fruit or rotten turnips, shake trees, and dig where you hear strange noises.

Fish are harder to determine than bugs, as you can only see how big the shadow is, but rare fish are often worth much more than a rare bug.

On the flipside, you can familiarize yourself with the rare bugs that should appear on your island during each month to know when to stop what you're doing to capture them.

If you stockpile fish and bugs, be on the lookout for Flick and CJ, who can appear on random days asking to buy critters for increased prices.

General Tips

There's a ton more you can and should be doing in ACNH, and a lot of interesting things you may not have noticed. If you've got a general tip, feel free suggest one in the comments!

Clear out any weeds that surround trees and rocks - items that fall from them need a place to land, and if weeds are in the way they bounce another space away - or disappear entirely if there's no room.

You can movie items around in your inventory by holding "A" hovering over the item you want to move.

Running through flowers won't destroy them anymore, but they will destroy the bulbs, requiring you to wait for them to bloom again.

Consider keeping a DIY workbench in your inventory if you're exploring the farther ends of your island. This way you can craft whatever tools you need should they break while you're exploring or gathering resources.

Check the recycle bin inside Nook Services (even if you're playing by yourself!) Items will appear from time to time.

You'll see various symbols in the crafting menu on the lower right side of a card. A box means the item is in your storage and the bag means it's in your inventory. If there's no symbol, you don't have that item in your possession. It does not account for furniture you've placed around the island.

Hold B to make dialogue go by faster.

You can toss items into trash cans you place around the island!

Don't sell big ticket items in the drop-off box unless you don't care about loosing Bells! They only sell for 80% of what they're worth due to fees.

You can bury holes in the ground with your foot by hitting "Y" when you're facing one.

If you have a stack of flowers you want to keep on you but out of your inventory, you can wear all 10 in a stack at once! (more of a neat thing) It won't look like you're wearing 10 flowers, though.

Lacking storage space in the first few days? You can place items outside while you wait for Blathers to show up, your house to be constructed, or Nook's Cranny to open. Don't worry, they won't go anywhere.

THINGS ANIMAL CROSSING: NEW HORIZONS DOESN'T TELL YOU

In case you're an Animal Crossing veteran, you most likely definitely know a lot of mysteries that make Animal Crossing life and Tom Nook obligation goal considerably simpler. Yet, there are many things that Animal Crossing: New Horizons simply doesn't tell you. We've gotten together a huge load of seemingly insignificant details New Horizons doesn't exactly tell you:

Hold B to run! You can likewise hold B to make any exchange pass by quicker

You can make making DIY projects go quicker by quickly squeezing the A Button!

On the off chance that your digging tool breaks, you can in any case stop up openings in the ground by squeezing Y. You can likewise jump over openings or little holes by running towards them.

Squeezing right or left on the D-Pad cycles between accessible instruments and held things - however you can likewise decide the request it cycles by modifying your stock: simply hold a to hold and drag a thing and submit them in the request you need. Press Down on the D - Pad to take care of your things.

In case there are weeds, rocks, or any arbitrary things on the ground, different things will not have the option to fall there - like branches - or furniture!- from a tree, just as assets chipped away from a stone. Ensure you clear the ground prior to attempting to gather materials.

Strike shakes up to 8 times each day by burrowing openings behind you to prevent yourself from getting thumped back. One arbitrary stone each day will really deliver ringers all things being equal!

When shaking trees for treats, here and there you'll get a wasp home all things being equal. Wasps will follow you, and make your face unrecognizable for an entire day, so hold a net out first prior to shaking a tree to get them before they sting you! On the off chance that they surprise you, you can likewise raise your stock - or press left and right on the D-Pad to upset the wasps briefly while you get your instrument.

The main player to begin the island (The Resident Representative) is the impetus for the vast majority of your town's movement and opening different offices by conversing with Tom Nook. Different players sharing the island will not have the option to start these occasions, yet they can assist with contributing once an errand has been given.

On the off chance that you do get stung, visit a resident - they'll show you how to make medication which will fix your revolting face. Uh, simply the part that was stung. Sorry. (Note that if your stock is full when this occurs, you may not get the formula - yet you can utilize one more record on your change to exchange yourself the formula)

You'll get a declaration from Resident Services every day - which will consistently start at 5am, or at whatever point you initially fire up your person after that.

Going through blossoms will not annihilate the whole plant, yet they can destroy the bulbs, which will require a couple of days to sprout once more. These parts can likewise be picked to wear or specialty into things.

Assuming you need to move blossoms to an alternate area, utilize a digging tool to relocate them. This should likewise be possible with trees, yet you'll have to eat some organic product first. Assuming that you're at any point befuddled with regards to what sort of trees are before you, get it and check out it in your stock to discover.

Eating organic product will likewise make you tear open rocks when hit with a digging tool. While this is useful for clearing land, you will not have the option to get assets from it after that. Fortunately, another stone will show up elsewhere on the island in a couple of days.

Need to change your look? Specialty or purchase furniture with a mirror, and you'll even have the option to pick between a couple of a larger number of haircuts than you began with. Get a closet or cabinet, and you can modify your apparel utilizing a jazzy interface.

When visiting a Villager's home, you can really utilize their studio or mirror as you would your own - in any event, in case they're not previously utilizing it.

Stone tomahawks can slash at a tree without wrecking it, permitting you to get three wood from it each day. An iron hatchet will slash down the tree after three swings - however certain bugs can appear on the stumps that you may not see in any case.

On the off chance that you see a Shooting Star in the sky, immediately press A to "wish" on it. The sections will appear on shore the following day, so ensure you find and get them.

Here and there you'll find meandering NPCs, try to look for them every day and talk with them.

Created things will sell for something beyond the plain materials - like weeds made into a Leaf Umbrella

Have you seen a gleaming spot on the ground? Uncover it to get a free 1,000 ringers! In case you're searching for a speculation, replant the chimes and you'll get triple the sum inside a couple of days when the tree is completely developed - however it just develops ringers once..

You'll see different images in the creating menu on the lower right half of a card:

A mark implies you've effectively made it previously.

A case implies the thing is in your capacity and the sack implies it's in your stock. In case there's no image, you don't have that thing in your ownership - however it doesn't represent the furniture you've put around the island.

When you figure out how to modify furniture, any thing that can be redone will have a paintbrush symbol.

Not all Nook Miles Challenges are shown when you have the right devices. Some of them are concealed until you've as of now finished the test - like getting 5 wasps in succession without getting stung.

You can put Custom Designs on an amazing measure of articles including PC screens (we purchased a Desktop Computer for 100K ringers).

Customization goes past paint and plans. For example, you can modify an Iron Pan to have food in it!

ABOUT THE AUTHOR

I When I finding new tricks, tips, and strategies to beat each other, they came up with a brilliant idea. Let's take these hours of gaming expertise, and share these skills with like mind people. At that moment, the Happy Home Paradise Guide were born. With more exciting gaming books being developed in the Lab as we speak. I am creating a buzz in the gaming guide publishing world, with a ground swell of followers, anxiously awaiting my new releases.

www.ingramcontent.com/pod-product-compliance
Ingram Content Group UK Ltd.
Pitfield, Milton Keynes, MK11 3LW, UK
UKHW022011190726
13853UKWH00004B/1864